Next place a weight such
Place stack in refrige

Next heat up 2 tablespoons of oil (Use a nonstick skillet, set to medium heat.

Now carefully remove ramen buns.(CAREFULLY!) from containers and place them in oil. Fry them until they are light brown and nice and crisp.

Turn your buns (You may add a little oil if needed.) Fry them up until brown on other side. Remove and drain off on paper towels. (One pack serves 1.)

Ramen Burger

Ingredients:

Makes 3 burgers Servings

- 2 Packages of instant ramen noodles, flavor packet discarded
- 2 Large size eggs (Mid size will do.)
- Salt and Pepper just for taste
- 3/4 pound lean ground beef (or ground beef.)
- 1-2 Tablespoons of soy sauce
- 1-2 Teaspoons of sesame oil
- 2-3 Tablespoons vegetable oil, divided
- 3 slices American cheese (or six slices for extra cheese.)
- 1/4 cup ketchup
- 2-3 tablespoons of chile-garlic sauce (I like Sriracha Hot Sauce.)
- 1-2 cups arugula
- 3 large eggs (set aside)

Directions

Start by boiling water in a pot; Now add your ramen noodles.
Boil, while stirring occasionally, or until noodles are nice and tender,
Cook this for about 3-4 minutes. Now drain everything. Allow your noodles to cool off.

Now beat 2 eggs in a bowl; You may season with salt and pepper if you like. Stir the noodles into your eggs or until bowl is coated. next go ahead and divide noodles into 4-6 burger-size rounds into bowls. Place a sheet of plastic wrap directly over noodles and stack bowls on top of each other to flatten out noodles.

Refrigerate the bowl until nice and firm, about 20-60 minutes.

While the noodles are cooling off mix ground beef,sesame oil, and soy sauce, in a bowl. Next divide beef mixture into patties. (about 4-6.)

Heat 1-2 tablespoons of vegetable oil, next place it into a large skillet set to medium-heat. Grab your cooled ramen and turn each ramen bowl over. Go ahead and gently tap bottom of the bowl. The ramen loosens, and carefully remove to maintain its bun shape.

Fry each ramen bun, (without moving noodles,) let it sit in oil until brown, do this for about 3 minutes.

Now flip each noodle bun, and fry the other side until crisp, 3 to 4 minutes more. Don't burn them (Noodles will look golden brown on each side.)

Should be crispy on one side, And softer on the other. move your noodle buns to large plate with crispy side up. (looking good so far!)

Heat up your 1-2 tablespoons of vegetable oil use the same skillet.(That you fried your ramen in.

Go ahead and start cooking up beef patties until burgers are cooked to liking.

Mix the ketchup in chile-garlic sauce in a small size bowl;

You may spread mixture on the crispy side of each ramen bun.

Next divide arugula over the ramen buns. Place burgers on top of arugula.

Heat about 1-2 teaspoons of oil in a skillet , fry the remaining eggs (one at a time.)

You can add a little more oil if needed, When yolk is almost firm, in about 1 minute or so per side. Place the egg over patty then add remaining noodle bun.

That's it your done enjoy!

Ramen Noodle Burger: Bok Choy

INGREDIENTS

1 packet Ramen noodles

2 eggs

7 oz. ground beef

2 scallions

A little soy sauce

Splash of sesame oil

1 head of bok choy

Tomato ketchup

A little hot sauce

Slice of American cheese (or what ever slice cheese.)

Splash of oil (For cooking.)

PREPARATION

Boil the noodles in a salted water bath according to instructions,

But don't add the seasoning packets. Drain all the water.

Now cook up your Ramen Buns, using the (**EASY RAMEN BUNS method at the beginning of book.)**

Next slice up the scallions then mix them into the beef, go ahead and add noodle seasoning, sesame oil, and soy sauce. Now form two burger patties, make them similar size as your buns, still keeping them pretty thin.

Heat up the three frying pans. Fry the burgers in one pan with a shot of oil for a minute or so on each side.

1. Remove the chilled ramen burger buns from the plastic wrap and fry in a shot of oil in the second pan for 2 minutes on each side so that they get golden and crispy.

2. Crack egg and fry in the third pan.

3. Mix together the ketchup and hot sauce.

Wash the bok choy then steam it very quickly in the pan (use only a dash of water.)

Drain everything place on paper towels to remove grease.

Ramen burger buns with a slices of cheese on top of each burger patty.

Arrange them any way you see fit.

Homemade Ramen Burger 3 (Bacon flavored)

Ingredients:

1 Pack of ramen noodles

1 egg any size

Burger ingredients:

Burger patty (frozen)

Curry powder (if you like)

Lettuce, Tomatoes, Spinach, etc

Bacon bits or any bacon flavored Onion Crunch

Cheese slice (optional)

Fried egg (To top)

1 teaspoon of butter

Directions:

START BY USING THE EASY RAMEN BUNS

Boil a pot of water. Add the noodles then the season packet. Cook the noodles until they are tender (but not too soft, cook for about 2 to 4 minutes. Now drain everything, and let cool down.

Now place the noodles in the bowl. Beat the eggs then pour it over the noodles, tossing it around to coat well.

Next divide the noodles into 2 plastic containers. Place them plastic wrap, (or baking parchment.)

Now place 1 container on top of the other.

Place 3rd container on top that stack.

Next place a weight such as a can of soup into the top container.

Place stack in refrigerator, and let chill about 1-2 hours.

Next heat up 2 tablespoons of oil (Use a nonstick skillet, set to medium heat.

Now carefully remove ramen buns.(CAREFULLY!) from containers and place them in oil. Fry them until they are light brown and nice and crisp.

Turn your buns (You may add a little oil if needed.) Fry them up until brown on other side. Remove and drain off on paper towels.

Start by heating up and/cooking your burger patty.

Make a free form patty with ground beef, curry powder and salt. To add more of a Japanese flare.

Heat your pan with a little oil and butter.

Flip over your ramen noodle container upside down so that the noodle bun slides easily into frying pan in one piece.

Fry for a few minutes on both sides until noodles become slightly crispy.

Add in patty and additional toppings of your choice.

RAMEN WAFFLE SANDWICH

The waffle will be soft inside with a little bit crunch along the edges.

Method:

Start by boiling the the ramen the usual way.

Drain . In a mixing bowl, whisk up 1 egg, 2 tablespoons white flour, 1/2 teaspoon baking powder, 2 tablespoons water, and 1/2 packet chicken flavoring.

Add the noodles and mix together. (Use your hands so you don't break them up.)

Now go ahead split the mixture in two sections into your waffle maker, and cook them on the darkest setting.

All done build your breakfast beast of a sandwich.

Ramen Turkey Burger 5

Ingredients

- 1 package ground turkey
- 1 tablespoon of soy sauce (Sub for teriyaki sauce if you like.)
- 1 tablespoon of minced garlic

- 1 tsp of chili pepper flakes
- Salt and pepper just for taste
- 1 pack of ramen noodles (1 for each burger.)
- 2 eggs (1 per burger .)
- Hot Sriracha sauce or (any hot sause.)
- Arugula
- Diced greed onion
- Sautéd red onion, or any other onion rings
- 1 tablespoon oil or (sesame oil.)

Take the first 5 ingredients then mix them all together. (Use a small- mid bowl.)

Make about 4 turkey hamburger patties. (Use your hands to make rounds.)

Grill up and fry them as desired.

Cook your ramen noodles the normal way just leave out the flavor packet.

Next drain your noodles.

Whisk up the eggs then coat your noodles.

Now separate the noodles in half. Place one half in one ramekin dish, the other half in a second ramekin dish. Place saran wrap over each dish and press the noodles down with a can of food or another bowl. Refrigerate for about 10-15 minutes.

Make your sriracha sauce by using half sriracha per half ketchup. Stir it all up.

Now to make the "buns", carefully place the noodle cakes into a medium/hot pan. Fry until golden brown on both sides. You have just made your buns.

Fry the egg over easy or over medium.

Time to assemble the turkey burgers.

Spread some sriracha ketchup on the bottom half of your noodle bun. Place a nice layer of arugula, then add the turkey hamburger patty on top. Next, go ahead and your cheese slice, then the fried egg, and onions (sauté, green onions). All done enjoy.

Vegan Eggplant Burger

Ingredients

Ramen Noodle Buns

- 4 ounces of ramen noodles
- 2 flax eggs (2 tablespoons of ground flax seed)
- 2 tablespoons green onion, sliced thin
- ¼ teaspoon salt
- ¼ teaspoon ground black pepper
- 1 teaspoon extra-virgin olive oil (or more)

Eggplant Burger

- 1 medium eggplant, peeled and diced into small cubes (approximately 3-3½ cups)
- ⅓ cup finely chopped red pepper
- 1 cup vegan bread crumbs (or more)
- 1 flax egg (1 tablespoon of ground flax seed)
- 1 shallot, minced
- 1 garlic clove, minced
- 1 teaspoon fresh chopped rosemary (or ½ teaspoon dried)

¼ teaspoon coriander

½ teaspoon oregano

½ teaspoon salt

1 tablespoon fresh squeezed lemon juice

¼ teaspoon ground black pepper

2 tablespoons fresh parsley, chopped

2 teaspoons of extra-virgin olive oil

Tahini Sauce

⅛ cup lemon juice

½ cup tahini paste (sesame-seed paste)

1 garlic clove, minced

¼ teaspoon salt

Couple of twists of fresh ground black pepper

Instructions

Tahini Sauce

Combine all sauce ingredients into a bowl and whisk until smooth. If too thick, add a little warm water a teaspoon at a time until desired consistency. Refrigerate.

RAMEN BUNS

1 package of dry ramen noodles, any flavor, will do. (I like Top Ramen Noodles.)

1 egg (Small size egg will do.)

3 round plastic containers, (Have them at about 4 inches diameter.)

2-3 tablespoons of Vegetable oil

Boil a pot of water. Add the noodles then the season packet. Cook the noodles until they are tender (but not too soft, cook for about 2 to 4 minutes.

Now drain everything, and let cool down.

Now place the noodles in the bowl. Beat the eggs then pour it over the noodles, tossing it around to coat well.

Next divide the noodles into 2 plastic containers. Place them plastic wrap, (or baking parchment.)

Now place 1 container on top of the other.

Place 3rd container on top that stack.

Next place a weight such as a can of soup into the top container.

Place stack in refrigerator, and let chill about 1-2 hours.

Next heat up 2 tablespoons of oil (Use a nonstick skillet, set to medium heat.

Now carefully remove ramen buns.(CAREFULLY!) from containers and place them in oil. Fry them until they are light brown and nice and crisp.

Turn your buns (You may add a little oil if needed.) Fry them up until brown on other side. Remove and drain off on paper towels. (One pack serves 1.)

Eggplant burger

Whisk together 1 tablespoon of ground flax seed and about 2-3 tablespoons of water. Refrigerate for the next 10 minutes or longer if needed.

Now grab a large non-stick skillet, lets heat up 1 teaspoon of oil set to medium-high heat. Add the eggplant cubes with red pepper. Saute them until the eggplant is brown nice and soft. (Add a little bit of vegetable broth if it starts to get sticky instead of adding more oil.)

Add the salt and pepper, shallot, rosemary, garlic, coriander and oregano. Cook for about 1-2 minutes. Taste and adjust your seasonings if needed.

Remove from pan and mash with a potato masher (If you have one) until completely crushed.

Add the bread crumbs to parsley , lemon juice, flax egg and combine them. (if needed add some more bread crumbs.)

Refrigerate covered for about 25-30 minutes or longer.

Heat oil set to medium-high heat in a large non-stick skillet.

(Get your hand wet so the mixture does not stick) Now useing your wet hands, divide up the eggplant mixture into about 4 burgers. Use your skillet to cook them until golden brown on each side.

Turn them very gently so they don't break.

Serve them on top of ramen noodle bun.

Drizzle with a little tahini sauce

Top the burgers with your favorite garnishes like: lettuce, tomatoes, vegan cheese, and red onion.

Here's a idea! Serve these little burgers in pita bread or lettuce wraps.

Ramen Hisago Burger

RAMEN BUNS

1 package of dry ramen noodles, any flavor, will do. (I like Top Ramen Noodles.)

1 egg (Small size egg will do.)

3 round plastic containers, (Have them at about 4 inches diameter.)

2-3 tablespoons of Vegetable oil

Boil a pot of water. Add the noodles then the season packet. Cook the noodles until they are tender (but not too soft, cook for about 2 to 4 minutes. Now drain everything, and let cool down.

Now place the noodles in the bowl. Beat the eggs then pour it over the noodles, tossing it around to coat well.

Next divide the noodles into 2 plastic containers. Place them plastic wrap, (or baking parchment.)

Now place 1 container on top of the other.

Place 3rd container on top that stack.

Next place a weight such as a can of soup into the top container.

Place stack in refrigerator, and let chill about 1-2 hours.

Next heat up 2 tablespoons of oil (Use a nonstick skillet, set to medium heat.

Now carefully remove ramen buns.(CAREFULLY!) from containers and place them in oil. Fry them until they are light brown and nice and crisp.

Turn your buns (You may add a little oil if needed.) Fry them up until brown on other side. Remove and drain off on paper towels. (One pack serves 1.)

Hisago Burger

    1-1/2 tablespoons dehydrated onion

    1/2 cup hot water

    4 slices white bread, torn in pieces

    2 pounds ground beef (80 percent lean)

    1-1/2 tablespoons minced celery

    1/4 teaspoon salt, or to taste

    1/4 teaspoon pepper, or to taste

    1 teaspoon vegetable oil

Cooking Process:

EASY RAMEN BUNS

1 package of dry ramen noodles, any flavor, will do. (I like Top Ramen Noodles.)

1 egg (Small size egg will do.)

3 round plastic containers, (Have them at about 4 inches diameter.)

2-3 tablespoons of Vegetable oil

Boil a pot of water. Add the noodles then the season packet. Cook the noodles until they are tender (but not too soft, cook for about 2 to 4 minutes. Now drain everything, and let cool down.

Now place the noodles in the bowl. Beat the eggs then pour it over the noodles, tossing it around to coat well.

Next divide the noodles into 2 plastic containers. Place them plastic wrap, (or baking parchment.)

Now place 1 container on top of the other.

Place 3rd container on top that stack.

Next place a weight such as a can of soup into the top container.

Place stack in refrigerator, and let chill about 1-2 hours.

Next heat up 2 tablespoons of oil (Use a nonstick skillet, set to medium heat.

Now carefully remove ramen buns.(CAREFULLY!) from containers and place them in oil. Fry them until they are light brown and nice and crisp.

Turn your buns (You may add a little oil if needed.) Fry them up until brown on other side. Remove and drain off on paper towels. (One pack serves 1.)

Hisago Delicatessen Burger

Soak onion in hot water until soft. Pour mixture over bread pieces and toss until bread falls apart and forms a soft paste (add more water if needed). Add beef, celery, salt and pepper; toss lightly to combine.

Form into 8 patties about 1 inch thick.

Here's a tip make a little depression in the center (This will help the burgers cook evenly).

Now put a little oil in skillet.

Fry the burgers set to medium-high heat cook them for about 5 minutes on each side.

If you would like to make sandwiches use: kalua pork, boneless teriyaki chicken, teriyaki hamburger patty (make sure it pre-cooked), 1 piece bulgogi, sliced up.

For the garnish add grilled onions, chopped green onion, arugula, BBQ sauce. All done enjoy!

BONUS BOOK
BEST Ramen Noodle Recipes
CLICK HERE TO GRAB A COPY:

http://www.amazon.com/dp/B00NSBLNXG

Broccoli and Ramen Noodle Salad

Ingredients:

- 1 package broccoli coleslaw mix (16-24 ounce)
- 2 packages of chicken flavored ramen noodles
- 1 bunch green onions, chopped
- 1 cup unsalted peanuts
- 1 cup sunflower seeds (No shells)
- 1/4 cup white sugar
- 1/4 cup vegetable oil
- 1/3 cup apple cider vinegar

Directions

Break up ad cook noodles, drain all the water.

Use a large salad bowl, and combine the slaw with green onions. Now add the broken noodles.

Whisk everything together: sugar, oil, vinegar and the two ramen chicken seasoning packets. Now pour over salad and toss to evenly coat. Refrigerate until cool; next top with peanuts and sunflower seeds before serving. All done!

Asian Noodles"n Shrimp

Ingredients

    1 can lite coconut milk

    2 cup of preshredded carrots

    1 medium size onion, (make sure you slice thinly.)

    12 ounce raw medium shrimp, peeled and deveined

    2 package shrimp-flavor ramen noodles (Set 1 seasoning pkt aside until needed.)

    2 cups of snow peas, (Make sure strings are removed)

    1/4 cup of finely chopped cilantro

    3 teaspoons of fresh lime juice

Directions

Bring two 1/4 cups of water, add the coconut milk, carrots and onion to a boil (Use 10 inch skillet is best.)

Next grab your snow peas, ramen noodles and shrimp; (press them down to submerge in juices.) Bring everything to a nice simmer and, stirring to break up noodles, simmer for about 2 to 4 minutes more or until shrimp are cooked through.

Remove from heat and stir in that extra seasoning packet, add cilantro and lime juice for taste. Now serve immediately.

Coconut Curry Shrimp

Ingredients

2 package ramen noodles (Any flavor will do but Shrimp is best)

1/2 cup light coconut milk

1/3 cup creamy peanut butter (Try nutty peanut butter for a extra crunch.)

2 tablespoons of fresh lime juice

1/4 teaspoon of crushed red pepper flakes (optional)

1 pound of cooked, large shrimp, cleaned, peeled (thawed out not frozen.)

1/2 cucumber, cut into thin half moon sizes

4 scallions, sliced diagonally or what ever way you like

4 Lime wedges, (Just for serving.)

Directions

Boil up 4 cups of water (large skillet is best.) Break each package of noodles into 4 sections if you can. Now add to boiling water (save the seasoning packets use them for something else). Cover skillet with lid, next remove from heat and sit for about 5 minutes.

While that's sitting, in a Mid-large bowl, whisk the lime juice , peanut butter, coconut milk, and red pepper.

Now drain the noodles. Add everything together into the bowl with the dressing.

After that add cucumber,shrimp, and scallions toss it up. Serve with a side of lime wedges.

Ramen'n Beef or Chicken with Veggies

4 packs of Ramen, (You may use any flavor.)

1 pound of Chicken or Beef. (If you use Tofu, make sure it serves 4 people.)

1 Cup Frozen Veggies, (Its your choice, anything you have.)

You may add shredded Cheese if you desire.

Sauté your meat or meats until done.

Next cook Ramen in just enough water to cover noodles. Now add frozen veggies to Ramen cook for 1 minute just before noodles are done.

Drain some of the water when Ramen is done,

The noodles should be a chunky soup, (a lot of water.) Then add flavoring packs, Place in large bowl, top with shredded cheese, if you want. You may serve with a side of bread.

All Done Enjoy!

Easy Noodle Salad

Ingredients:

Servings: 4-6 people

    1 bag coleslaw mix about 16oz

    1 package ramen noodles, raw & crushed (Any flavor)

    1/2 cup sunflower seeds (no shells.)

1/2 cup oil (olive is best)

1/4 cup Apple cider vinegar

1/4 cup sugar (Sub for 6 packs of Splenda.)

Directions:

1. Mix together the coleslaw mix, crushed noodles& sunflower kernels.

2. In a small- mid size bowl, mix the Ramen Noodle seasoning packs.

3. Next add,oil, vinegar& sugar together.

4. Mix everything together and refrigerate at least 1-2 hours

5. All done! How easy was that?

Ramen Noodle Casserole

Ingredients

1 lb ground chuck

1 small -medium size onion , (Diced up.)

1 cup of diced tomatoes

3 packages beef-flavor ramen noodles

2-3 cups water

You may add Velveeta cheese, just for taste.

Instructions

Cook the Hamburger and onion until brown , Next add your 3 flavoring packets and simmer for about 4 minutes.

Add a 1/2cup water + tomatoes and bring them both to a boil.

Next add your noodles and cook them for about 3-4 minutes longer.

After that pour into a casserole dish,(make sure you spray it with cooking spray.) Now cover with sliced Velveeta cheese or any cheese you have.

Place it in the oven and bake for 15 minutes set to 325-350°

When cheese is melted your done. That's it enjoy!

Grilled Ramen

1 tbs Rice wine vinegar

2 tbs of Sesame oil

Take a ramen block, marinate it for about 20 minutes in things like rice wine vinegar and sesame oil, then grill it for 3 minutes on each side.

You may serve it alone, or add in some grilled vegetables.

Taking your BBQ to a whole new level.

Cheesy Baked Ramen (macaroni and cheese of ramen)

Boxed macaroni and cheese (Powder or Packed cheese)

If you don't have that use cheese-in-a-can

Shredded Cheese

Boil your Ramen to taste, next just add boxed cheese while Noodles are still warm.

Add in a little butter if your noodles start to stick. Mix everything up and top with Shredded Cheese. That's it!

Ramen Spam/ HAM

Ingredients:

    2 packages of chicken ramen noodles, (Make sure you break them up up slightly)

    3-4 cups of water

    1 can of spam, or canned ham (Diced them up in small cubes)

    1/4 cup of green peas

    1/4 cup of green onions, (slice them up)

    1 teaspoon garlic powder or 1/4 teaspoon of garlic salt

    1 tablespoon sesame oil

In a medium size pan, boil over set to high heat.

Next add the two packages of ramen noodles, and peas.

Cook for about 2-3 minutes, Now drain everything.

Now while noodles are cooking, heat up the sesame oil (use a small frying pan), add in spam cubes and green onion, stirring everything up occasionally to brown up the cubes.

After they are nice and browned add everything to the frying pan,

Next add the two seasoning packets, garlic powder or garlic salt, Start mixing well. That's it your ready to serve!

CHICKEN BROCCOLI NOODLES

2 pkgs. (3 oz. each) Ramen Pride chicken flavor Ramen noodle soup
1 can (10 3/4 oz.) Campbell's condensed cream of mushroom soup
1/2 soup can milk
1 c. cubed cooked chicken
1 c. cooked broccoli flowerets

Prepare Ramen noodle soup according to package directions. Add seasoning packets; drain most of the liquid. Stir in mushroom soup and milk. Add chicken and broccoli. Heat through. Makes 5 1/2 cups.

MARINATED NOODLES AND CABBAGE

1 (3 oz.) pkg. Oriental noodles with chicken flavor, like Top Ramen
1/4 cup oil
3 tbsp. rice vinegar
1 tbsp. sugar
1/4 tsp. salt
2 cup finely shredded cabbage
1 (6 3/4 oz.) can chunk-style chicken, drained

1/4 cup sliced green onion

3 tbsp. fried sesame seed

3 tbsp. sliced almonds, toasted

Green pepper cut into rings

Break the noodles up.

In a mixing bowl combine the ramen seasoning packet then mix with vinegar,oil, sugar, 1/4 teaspoon salt and dash of pepper.

Stir to dissolve up all the seasonings.

Stir in broken noodles, cabbage, chicken, onion and sesame seed.

Cover it up.

Chill it for a few hours. Now before you start serving stir in the almonds, and garnish it off with some green peppers rings. Looks so nice and taste so good!

TOP RAMEN NOODLE COLE SLAW

4 tbsp. sugar

2 tsp. salt

1 tsp. pepper

1/3 c. vinegar

2/3 c. Miracle Whip

1 med. head cabbage

5 green onions (optional)

8 tbsp. slivered almonds, toasted

8 tbsp. sesame seeds, toasted

1 can crushed pineapple, drained

Top Ramen noodles, broken

Seasonings from noodles

Prepare the dressing ahead of time and refrigerate over night.

Next mix up sugar,pepper, salt, vinegar and seasoning on top of the noodles,

Heat everything until sugar dissolves. Let it sit for a while until nice and cool.

Next add Miracle Whip and mix up well. Refrigerate for about 1-2 hours.

Shred some cabbage up fine, then add onions.

Good ahead and add your dressing, .

The last thing you need to do is add the broken noodles, almonds, sesame seeds, and pineapple.

Serves 10 to 12 people. (WOW!)

RAMEN NOODLE TACOS (YES TACOS!!!)

2 pkg. of Beef Ramen noodles or (any brand)

1 lb. Ground Beef or Ground Chicken / Turkey

1/2 head of Lettuce - Chopped up into fine slices

Cheese - (Shredded 3 cheese taco mix is best)

2 Tomatoes

Any other taco toppings you want to add

Taco shells

Taco sauce

Taco season pack.

Cook the noodles normal according to package ,

Don't add beef seasoning packets to noodles.(Place them aside)

Cook ground beef until nice and Brown. When done drain the juices.

Go ahead and grab the 2 beef packs and mix with beef. You may top with cheese at this time if you like. Drain noodles.

To make tacos:

Place the cut lettuce on serving plate.

Layer noodles on bottom of shell, then add beef.

Add any other taco toppings on top.

ALL DONE THAT"S IT!

EASY ORIENTAL NOODLE SALAD

1 head of cabbage shredded (or buy per packed shredded cabbage.)

6 scallions

1 1/2 cup. toasted almond slivers

4 tablespoon. sesame seeds (You may roast them at 350 degrees for about 4-5 minutes)

2 package of Ramen noodles (Make sure you crush them up)

Blend everything the ingredients and the dressing.

Now let's make the DRESSING:

2/3 oil

5 tablespoon. Apple cider vinegar or reg vinegar will do

3/4 tsp. salt

3/4 tsp. pepper

2 pkgs flavor packs from noodles

1 tablespoon. sugar or sugar sub

Mix everything up and now you have a nice dressing.

SESAME-NOODLE SHRIMP SALAD

1/3 cup rice vinegar

1/4 cup vegetable oil

2 tablespoon. sugar

1 garlic clove, minced up very fine

1/2 teaspoon. salt

2 teaspoon. soy sauce (any brand will do!)

1 teaspoon of sesame seed oil

1 teaspoon. hot chili paste (If you want)

1 teaspoon. sesame seeds, (Best if toasted)

SALAD:

2 pkgs. Ramen (Any flavor,)

1/2 lb. cooked lg. shrimp, peeled, and deveined (Save money by using salad shrimp)

2 cup finely shredded purple cabbage

2-3 thin green onions, smashed flat then shredded

1/3 cup slivered almonds, toasted

2-3 tbsp. fresh coriander leaves, shredded

Prepare dressing by mixing together all ingredients - then set aside.

Japan Like a PRO

Ingredients

Noodles

- 9 oz fresh angel hair pasta or 1 Ramen pack
- 8 cups water (2L)
- 2 Tbsp baking soda

Salted pork

- 1 lb pork
- 1 tsp salt

Soup

- 5-6 cups water
- 50grams of ginger root, (Make sure its sliced up good)
- 2-3 cloves garlic, (Cut and skinned)
- 1 Bunch green onions
- 4 Tablespoons soy sauce

2 Tablespoons sake

1 teaspoon salt

1 teaspoon sesame oil

Topping

Boiled a few egg halves

Bean sprouts, Have them blanched briefly

Green onions, cut them up finely

Instructions

Start by rubbing salt on the pork, Now it let it sit overnight placed in the fridge.

In a pot, put water, ginger root, garlic, green onions and salted pork, and boil set to high heat.

Make sure you Skim the fat, and any floating crap.

Next cover it up, and reduce to low heat, and simmer this for about 1 - 2 hours.

When ready let the broth pork cool down completely. (Let it rest in the pot)

Strain the pot, and remove pork.

Slice the pork, now set it aside for a topping later on.

Moving on get ready to prepare the rest of the toppings as well add the.

(blanched bean sprouts, boiled eggs, cut green onions), Do this before making soup and noodles.

Once the noodles are cooked, you will need to add your soup and toppings right away. (If you wait to long the noodles will get soft.) Then game over! If this happens grab a fresh pack and start cooking them over.

Boil the broth and adding soy sauce, salt, sake, and sesame oil.

Let it simmer set to low heat until noodles are ready.

Don't worry the next part is easy!

Now in a boiling pot of water, (Keep a eye on it, may boil over), then add the Ramen. Cook your pasta for 30 seconds, and strain.

Next Quickly divide noodles into bowls.

Now add the soup onto noodles. Top with bean sprouts, boiled eggs, green onions and sliced pork. ALL DONE!

BONUS BOOK: BY FAT MAN SCOOP:

Famous Backyard BBQ Recipes

(Easy Backyard Grilling Recipes) [Kindle Edition]

NEW UPDATE: MORE RECIPES ADDED 7-3-2014

By:

Ryan O Williams

First Edition, Published By Ryan O Williams

Copyright 2014, Row Books

This book is licensed for your personal enjoyment only. It may not be resold or shared if you would

like to share please purchase a second copy. All work in this book is a work of fiction. Any names or similar real life persons or actual places ,and br,ands are fictitious.

All rights reserved.

Thank you for purchasing Famous Backyard BBQ Recipes.

Ever since I was a little boy, I have always wondered why my father would BBQ in the winter. Now that I am older, I underst,and. He just couldn't wait till spring, to sink his teeth into a nice juicy steak or baby back ribs. With snow on the ground, the small of BBQ filled the air. As a gift he would package a few ,and give to neighbors. With mouths watered, ,and open arms they all loved a good BBQ. When got older, much older I decided to have a BBQ of my own. After moving into a new neighborhood, I wanted to invite a few people to my house-warming BBQ party.

With a nice size backyard, it was the perfect setting for tasty BBQ. To make a long story short it didn't turn out as I expected.

Burnt burgers, uncooked pork, bloody chicken. Thank God no one got sick! Maybe because no one really ate a thing. I so embarrassed! Didn't have many BBQ's after that.

I needed to fix this, my reputation was shattered. As a guy BBQ was supposed to be my thing. Over the years I got better ,and better. With many failed meats, ,and money burnt away.

I learned a few tips from my father. In which I will share with you in this book. Going to BBQ computation's watching, learning ,and taking notes. I was going to become The Master of BBQ.

After gaining more trust people decided to try my food once more.

"This taste great!"

"WOW!"

"Oh my Gosh!"

What did you put in this?

With trophies, ,and pictures of winning BBQ computations.

People now ask me if they could come to my BBQ. Even offer to pay for the foods. In this book I open my famous book of recipes. Your taste buds will sing, your mouth will water.

Your stomach will beg for more. No you don't need a fancy two thous,and dollar grill. I will teach you step by step. On how to make the best BBQ meals known to man.

With out further Adieu!

"Lets get started!"

Tools of the trade.

Like good car mechanic needs tools, each tool has a certain job.

Trust me a good set of BBQ gear goes a long way. I have many sets, but I prefer ones that come with a stainless steel lock box.

Most cost about $20-$30, ,and last a very long time if you keep them clean. Try A 18 Piece Deluxe BBQ Tool Set A good site is http://www.bbq-tools.com/

Food Preparation:

You may have to prepare your food before you grill it. Meat tenderizers, sauces, marinades. The night before is best, this will allow the marinades to soak into the meats.

But what type of grill should I get?

(Wood burning, Charcoal or Propane)

It does not really matter what grill you have. They all do the same job, but each has their own flavor. But that's up to you!

To save money Charcoal is the cheapest grill to buy. But the down side is the charcoal avg around $5-$15 per bag. If you do very little grilling then this maybe the way to go.

Propane grills cost around $100+ ,and tanks are $50 but refills cost about $20. the good thing about propane grill is the fact that you can grill many times. About 20-30 grills on one tank.

Like Charcoal wood burning cost about the same, but certain flavored wood cost $5-$20 per stack. (You can use your own wood but underst,and that flavor may change)

The Greatest Ever Juicy juice Burger

INGREDIENTS

    1/4 cup Mayonnaise

    1/2 cup plain dry bread crumbs

    1 Onion Soup Mix

    2 lbs. ground beef [or ground turkey]

    1/2 cup finely chopped red onion

    8 hamburger buns

Directions

    Go ahead ,and combine the Mayonnaise, bread crumbs ,and Soup Mix in bowl.

    mix up the mayonnaise mixture into ground beef; shape into 8 patties.

    GRILL or broil until done. Serve burgers on buns.

    The faster you eat, the faster you could grab another.

The SPIKE BURGER

INGREDIENTS

    1 & 1/2 pound Ground Beef [or ground turkey]

    1/4 cup finely chopped red onion

    4 of tablespoons barbecue sauce

    4 slices white Cheddar with pepper Jack ,and smoked Gouda or try provolone cheese

    4 whole wheat hamburger buns or any rolls, split, (toasted)

    Lettuce leaves, tomato slices ,and red onion slices

Lets Grill

    Combine the Ground Beef, onion ,and 2 tablespoons barbecue sauce in medium bowl, mixing lightly but thoroughly. Shape them into four 1/2-inch thick patties.

    Place patties on grid with medium heat, ash-covered coals. Grill, covered, 8 to 10 minutes (over medium heat on preheated your grill, for 8 - 10 minutes) or until instant-read thermometer inserted horizontally into center registers 160°F, turning occasionally. About 1 minute before burgers are done, you may brush on 2 tablespoons barbecue sauce ,then top with cheese.

Line bottom half of each bun with lettuce leaves, tomato ,and red onion slices, as desired; top with burger. Then Close s,andwiches. All done take big bites filling your mouth let the barbecue sauce drip down your shirt.

GRILLED T-BONE STEAKS WITH Rub A Dub

INGREDIENTS

2 to 6 beef T-Bone or Porterhouse Steaks, cut each one 1 inch thick

Pinch of Salt for each

BBQ Rub a dub:

- 2 tablespoons chili powder
- 3 tablespoons packed brown sugar
- 1 tablespoon ground cumin
- 2 teaspoons minced garlic
- 2 teaspoons cider vinegar
- 1 teaspoon Worcestershire sauce

1/4 teaspoon ground red pepper

Combine some BBQ Rub ingredients ,and press evenly onto beef steaks.

Place steaks on metal grid with medium, ash-covered coals. Grill, covered, 8 to 14 minutes (over medium heat on preheated gas grill, 8 to 10 minutes) for medium rare (145°F) to medium (160°F) doneness, turning occasionally. Remove bones ,and carve steaks into slices, if desired. Season with salt, as needed. Stack all the removed bones into a bowl ,and suck off any remaining meat. Lets not let any meat get away from our stomach.

The Whole Damn Chicken

INGREDIENTS:

2 whole chickens (about 3 lb. each)

2 small lemons, cut them in half

1 cup Baby Ray Original Barbecue Sauce

1 tsp. Italian seasoning

4 cloves garlic, peeled

Let's Grill

Start off by heating grill for indirect grilling. Light one side of the grill, while leaving other side unlit.

www.ingramcontent.com/pod-product-compliance
Lightning Source LLC
LaVergne TN
LVHW091410301224
800236LV00009B/304